British Library Cataloguing in Publication Data
Olesen, Jens
   Bumblebee.—(Stopwatch books).
   1. Bumblebees—Juvenile literature
   I. Title   II. Series
   595.79'9   QL568.A6

   ISBN 0–7136–2976–2

Published by A & C Black (Publishers) Limited
35 Bedford Row, London WC1R 4JH

This edition © 1988 A & C Black (Publishers) Limited
First published 1988 by Forlaget Apostrof, Copenhagen, Denmark
© 1988 Forlaget Apostrof

Acknowledgements
The illustrations are by Cathy Wood.
The publishers would like to thank Michael Chinery for his help and advice.

Filmset by August Filmsetting, Haydock, St. Helens.
Printed in Hong Kong by Dai Nippon Printing Co. Ltd.

Bumblebee

Jens Olesen
Photography by Bo Jarner

A & C Black · London

Here is a bumblebee.

Have you ever seen a bumblebee? The bumblebee in the big photograph is going to feed from a flower.

In spring, bumblebees make a nest under the ground. This bumblebee has found a hole where a mouse used to live. It will be a safe place for a nest.

This book will tell you what happens in a bumblebee's nest.

The queen bumblebee makes a nest.

These bumblebees are inside their nest under the ground.
The big bee is a queen bee. She made the nest.

In spring and summer, the queen bee lays hundreds of eggs.
The eggs develop into worker bees. Here is a queen bee
next to a worker bee.

queen   worker

Look at the photograph. The two small bees are worker bees.
The brown cases underneath the bees are called cocoons.
Inside some of the cocoons, more worker bees are growing.
The worker bees help the queen to look after the growing bees.

4

The queen bumblebee lays some eggs.

In the big photograph, the queen is laying some eggs.
Inside the yellow lumps, worker bees are already growing.

The queen lays her eggs inside a cup of wax. She makes
the wax inside her body.

These eggs are shown very large. In real life, each egg is
about as long as three full stops. When the queen has laid
her eggs, she covers them with some more wax.

The queen bumblebee keeps her eggs warm.

Look at the photograph. The queen bumblebee is lying
on top of the wax cup of eggs. This keeps the eggs warm.
If the eggs get cold, they will not hatch.

Can you see the wax cup of eggs in the drawing?
It is on top of some cocoons.

Grubs come out of the eggs.

After about five days, a white grub comes out of each egg. Here is a drawing of a grub.

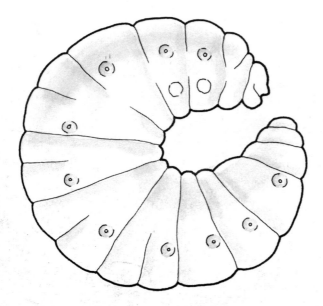

The grub has no eyes, no legs and no wings.

Look at the photograph. Can you see some grubs? The queen and the workers feed the grubs and they grow bigger every day.

The worker bees collect nectar from flowers.

The worker bees collect food from flowers and carry
it back to the nest.

This worker is sucking up a sugary liquid called nectar.
Can you see her tongue? It is a bit like a straw.

Look at the big photograph. The worker is putting nectar from
her stomach into a pot of wax, which is called a honeypot.

Later, the workers or the queen will feed some of the nectar
to the grubs.

The worker bees collect pollen from flowers.

When a worker bee lands on a flower, she gets a yellow dust called pollen in her fur. Look at the drawing.

The worker bee has rows of large hairs on her back legs. She packs the pollen between the hairs. Then she flies back to the nest.

Look at the photograph. Can you see a worker that looks as if she is wearing yellow trousers? She has lots of pollen on her legs. The pollen is food for the grubs.

Each grub changes into a pupa.

The grubs feed for about twelve days. Then each grub makes a neat, rounded cocoon out of silk. Can you see some of these round cocoons in the photograph?
Inside its cocoon, each grub changes into a pupa.

In the drawing, the cocoon has been cut in half so you can see what the pupa looks like.

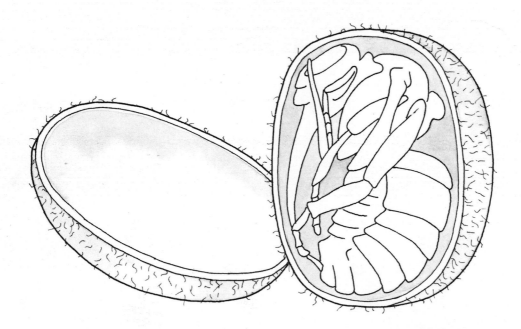

Over the next two weeks, the pupa slowly changes into an adult worker bee.

Worker bees come out of the cocoons.

When the worker bee is fully grown, she bites off the top of her cocoon.

Look at the big photograph. This worker bee has just come out of her cocoon. Her body is pale and soft but in a few hours she will look like the other workers.

New queen bees hatch out and find a mate.

At the end of summer, some of the grubs change into male bees. They are called drones. Later, other grubs change into new queen bees.

The drones and the new queen bees fly out of the nest. Each drone looks for a new queen to mate with.

Look at the photograph. This new queen is mating with a drone. Next spring, she will be able to lay eggs that turn into worker bees.

The new queen bees sleep through the winter.

In autumn, the old queen bee, the workers and the drones all die. But the new queen bees live until the next year.

Look at the photograph. This new queen bee is going to dig a burrow in the soil. All through the cold winter, the queen sleeps in her burrow.

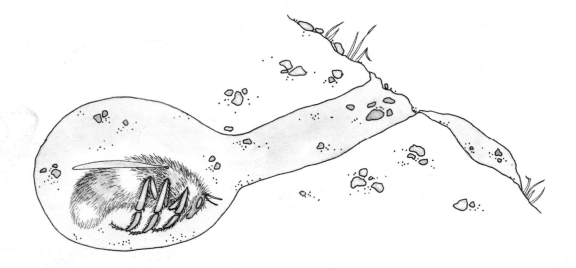

When spring comes, she will wake up and look for a place to build a nest.

What do you think will happen then?

Do you remember how the bumblebee came from the egg?
See if you can tell the story in your own words.
You can use these pictures to help you.

Index

This index will help you to find some of the important words in the book.

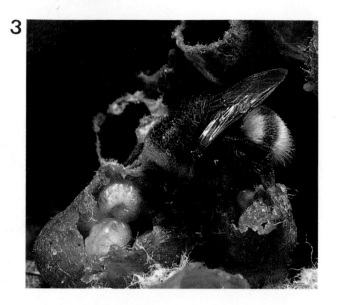

3

6

Watch a bumblebee visiting the flowers in a park or garden.
See if you can spot the yellow lumps of pollen on its back legs.
Try and see its tongue poking into the flowers to suck up nectar.